SEPARATED LIVES

Lynn Assimacopoulos

Writers' Branding
(877) 608-6550
www.writersbranding.com
media@writersbranding.com

Contents

Chapter One

It was spring when I first heard about Ryan. Our son Paul, who had moved to Long Beach, California, called to tell me he was working with a friend named Ryan Chadwell, who had been adopted as an infant. In the last couple of years, both of Ryan's adoptive parents had passed away in a car accident and Ryan felt quite lost. He had loved his adoptive parents dearly and had two adopted sisters; however, he did not know of any actual blood relatives.

Now in his early thirties, Ryan wanted to find out about his birthparents. New York City had been his home all of his life, and he had only recently moved to Long Beach.

While living in New York, Ryan's adoptive mother had taken him, a curious eight year old, to the adoption agency and helped him get any information available at that time. He had received a letter ten years earlier from the agency, containing only what was called "non-identifying information," which is all the law allowed. His mother had once taken him to the public library to find out any other possible information about his birth. Still, all they could find was minimal birth information. Ryan had also been to the genealogy room at the library, where he had discovered that his name at birth was Daniel Carter, his birthmother's name was Joyce Carter, and his birthfather's first name was Joel. Ryan suspected his birthfather probably did not even know he existed and guessed it would probably be easier to find his birthmother rather than his birthfather.

My son Paul knew I had extensively worked on our own family genealogy going back to the 1500s. He somehow thought maybe there was some way I could help guide Ryan in his search for his birthparents. Paul asked if I was willing to correspond with Ryan through email to give him some suggestions.

I consented, reminding Paul that I could not guarantee or promise anything since I was only an amateur genealogist, not a detective. I also told him it could turn out that Ryan's birthmother may not want to have any contact now, and since this would be her right, I felt I would have to respect that.

In a few days, I received an email from Ryan thanking me for my willingness to help him and maybe offer some suggestions. He told me he had been struggling with wanting to know who his birthparents were since he was eight years old, and he was adopted by two incredible people who raised him, fed him, clothed him, and loved him. He went on to say sadly, it was true his adoptive parents had both passed away in a car accident. While they were still living, they were vastly supportive of him searching for his birthparents.

He explained further that he was not trying to replace his deceased adoptive parents; he was just curious about his birth circumstances. He told me the institution where the adoption took place was the New York Foundling Hospital, and he told me his date of birth, adding that he would email me some information as well as "snail mail" copies of the papers he had previously obtained from this institution. I guessed it would probably be interesting, yet I was not very hopeful I could easily begin a search for what seemed something almost impossible, and especially in an enormous place like New York City. I had found out from researching my own family tree it was easier to find the deceased rather than the living due to the fact addresses, maiden names, marriage records, and other such information is greatly protected when a person is still alive. Of course, this is good for privacy's sake, yet not very good for a birthparent search.

A few weeks later, Ryan's papers arrived in the mail. I admit I was eager to look at them. On the letterhead he had obtained ten years ago was the name of the hospital where he was born. Just reading those words tugged at my heart. The letter was informing Ryan of the "non-identifying background and medical information" which he had requested.

It stated his mother, named Joyce Carter at the time, had been in her early twenties and single. She was Protestant, Caucasian, and of Danish ancestry, born and raised in the United States, a high school graduate who had attended one year of college and worked as a hotel receptionist. Her description was she was of average build, five feet, two inches tall, weighing one hundred ten pounds. She had blue eyes, short blond hair, and a fair complexion.

Medical information stated she was of B positive blood type, prone to sinus infections, and had a chronic condition of asthma. In addition, at age seven she had her tonsils out, and at age seventeen she had knee surgery on her right knee. Regarding his mother's parents, her father was a retired fireman and her mother had died of cancer in her fifties.

Ryan's birthfather was in his early twenties, single, Protestant, Caucasian, and of English heritage, born and raised in the United States. He was a man of average build and had brown hair, blue eyes, and a fair complexion. His employment was with a business machine company, and he was also a college student majoring in mathematics. One statement which stood out was "he was unaware of the pregnancy." Regarding his birthfather's parents, it only stated his father worked as a postmaster, and his mother was a psychologist.

The second page of the letter gave information about the date and time of Ryan's birth, along with his weight and length, stating the birth had been a normal delivery without any complications. What was sadly interesting was information on how Ryan's mother felt about the birth. She had stated adoption had always been her plan; still, she did this with a great deal of feeling and she did love him. Realistically she felt that it would be impractical for her to establish a home for him, since she was single and unprepared to deal with maternal responsibilities. She regarded herself as being too young to raise a child. She believed it would be wrong to deprive her child of a secure home and family and felt it would be socially unacceptable to keep him. She expressed that she placed great value on a two-parent home to provide love and security for a child. The letter went on to explain a little over a month after Ryan was born, he was baptized and admitted to the Foundling Hospital. Six months later, his mother "signed surrender." A month later, Ryan was placed in his adoptive parents' home for what was called "a view of legal adoption." One more month later, Ryan was legally adopted though the court system. Tears welled up in my eyes, thinking of my own three boys and wondering if I could have ever done this after their birth.

The letter ended with a statement of apology for the fact there was no more in the record to tell. It did state that if Ryan was interested in a possible reunion, there were some known adoption registries he could contact if he wished. A reunion could only take place if his birthmother had voluntarily registered with these same agencies. Both Ryan and I suspected she did not.

That was it. All Ryan knew about when his life began was condensed into a page and a half. How sad this made me feel. Could I possibly imagine how Ryan must have felt when he read these pages? After all, most of us know quite a bit about our parents and grandparents: where they lived, what they did with their lives, and most of all they loved us, watched us grow up, and tried to help us. Quickly my thoughts again turned to how excited and happy I was each time when my three sons were born. I still remember seeing their tiny faces for the first time looking up at me from the baby blue hospital blanket. Could I possibly have held them and then turned them away, knowing I would never see them again? It was easy for me to think I could have never done that; however, I know it is tremendously unfair to judge someone else since I have never been in the same situation.

Many questions began flooding into my thoughts. Where was she now? Was she married? Did she have other children? Did she ever think of Ryan? Did she ever tell anyone about him? Finally, I wondered: would she ever be found by me? When Mother's Day came around, I thought a lot about the search for Ryan's mother, and I emailed both my son and Ryan. I told Ryan I was going to consider myself his adoptive mother until if and when we found his real birthmother. I told my son he now had another brother for the time being. I was determined that somehow, some way, I still might be able to find Ryan's birthmother.

Chapter Two

It was now summer, and my husband and I planned to take a vacation to Long Beach to visit our son Paul. This would be my first chance to actually meet Ryan in person. I must admit I was anxious to see how the "email Ryan" compared to the "in-person Ryan." After we arrived, Ryan invited us all to lunch at his apartment. I found him much more interesting in person than I expected. Pleasant and friendly, he had a clever sense of humor and was full of witty statements. He was gracious and grateful that I was interested in helping him with the search for his birthmother. I could not help thinking of what his birthmother was missing, and this visit certainly prodded me on to continue the search.

After we left, I could not keep one item out of my mind. It was a basket on Ryan's desk which he had filled with items from nature, such as feathers, natural pieces of wood, rocks, fossils, and other artifacts. I had asked him what this basket meant and why he filled it with those objects. He said he really didn't have a reason, he just liked it. When I returned home, I emailed Ryan telling him I thought the basket meant something to our search. I really had no idea what it meant at the time. I just felt it meant something. He agreed we both would make it a point to remember the basket if some related connection came to us during our search.

In the next few months into the fall, my email was flooded with conversations between Ryan and me. The more information I received, the more interesting his situation sounded to me. He had a knack of using words in an interesting way, which I liked. He seemed as genuinely serious about the search as I was, and we both confessed that we loved a good mystery, agreeing we certainly were beginning some kind of a journey into one.

I had already made the decision to help with Ryan's search, but I hadn't yet had one particular serious discussion with Ryan. I sincerely felt compelled to tell him it would be necessary that both he and I face the fact if by some miracle I found his birthmother, there was a likely possibility she may not have wanted to be found. Also, she may not now or ever want to hear from him or have anything to do with him. It sounded rather harsh, but I felt this could possibly happen. What if she had another family and another life now? After all, I was a mother myself. I tried to imagine how I might handle this if I was in the same situation. I told him that if I did find her, I would only (and I meant only) give him the information if she consented. I felt I could not do this on any other terms. She may well feel strongly about putting that situation in the past and leaving it there. I was treading on tremendous private issues. I needed to be fair. Ryan understood this and agreed. I felt relieved.

Not really knowing exactly where or how to begin, it seemed logical to think about what I did know, like all the facts and information about the time and his birth in the New York City area. Of course, who was I kidding? I knew absolutely nothing about New York City. I also had to decide what I was going to ask, since at least right now, I didn't want to divulge the true reason I was looking for Ryan's birthparents. Not yet. I felt I could not disclose much at the beginning of the search just in case there was the possibility I would find his birthmother and she did not want to be found. I decided to search on the premise that I was researching a family tree for someone.

I began by using the wonderful invention of the computer. Since I was computer-illiterate for most of my life, way into my fifties, and only then compelled to learn "computer-ese," or as some may call it "Computers 101," at one of my jobs. Now I was certainly grateful and much indebted to computers as well as the internet. In my thirties I had done my own family genealogy without such technology and was forced to suffer through the use of pencil, paper, mail inquiries, telephone calls, and visiting cemeteries.

Now, using the internet, I could search New York City phone listings and addresses of persons with the same last name as Ryan's birthmother's, Carter, thinking maybe she still had relatives around in the same area. After finding some addresses, I mailed about one hundred letters of inquiry, starting with addresses right in New York City and working towards the outskirts. Still feeling I could not really explain the exact true nature of my search, I instead stated in these letters that I was working on some genealogical research on the Carter name and was specifically looking for a person who was believed to have lived in New York City in the 1960s. I explained I had found their Carter name in telephone listings on the internet and wanted to know if they had any information on a Joyce Carter, adding only a few details, such as her birth year, her Danish descent, and her religious affiliation as Protestant. I did not know her parents' first names. I knew her mother had died in her fifties. Her father was a retired fireman some time before the midsixties, and I did not know where. I did know that Joyce Carter had lived and worked in New York City when she was in her early twenties. Whether she had any brothers or sisters I also didn't know. I ended the letter by telling them they did not have to feel obligated to answer my letter unless they actually had information which may be of interest to my search. It was not too surprising when there were very few responses, although some persons were kind enough to respond anyway, stating that they did not know that particular name. I even wrote to several Protestant churches in the area, thinking maybe she might still be attending one of them.

These first search efforts were entirely fruitless; therefore, I ended up with no more information than when I started. I was not about to give up yet. I was about to just begin to fire my computer up on the internet once again!

Later I began to look for family trees and genealogical sites on the internet. Searching in all the genealogical message and bulletin boards I could find, I placed my own message about who I was searching for. To my amazement, I found many helpful persons who were also working on genealogy. From those people I received some nice responses with more suggestions for searching various places on the internet. Constantly I was telling myself she had to be somewhere. I also had to keep reminding myself one of the problems was she most likely was married now, and I didn't know or have a married name.

Chapter Three

Later, a surprising opportunity presented itself that might allow me to pursue a new avenue of searching. I was planning to attend a professional nursing conference in Washington, DC. I was going to make a visit to the National Archives, where there existed an enormous amount of genealogical records and information. This was extremely exciting, because having never been there, I had heard much about it. I was certain there would be some kind of information that I could use. Little did I know that my excitement would pretty much be squelched as soon as I walked through the door of the archives. When I spoke with a very experienced genealogical worker at the archives, he told me it was impossible to find anyone with the minimal amount of information I had. He advised me that I might as well give up on finding Ryan's mother since there was a tremendous amount of difficulty in finding female persons who had changed their name by marriage.

Despite my disappointment and his discouragement, I was not ready to give up. I was a stubborn Norwegian! I had found information in my own family tree which no one ever expected me to find either, which surprised even my own relatives.

During the next few months, I nearly exhausted what I thought were all my resources to help find Ryan's birthmother, and I still did not want to give up. For months I had been writing and searching any place I could think of, trying to find any available information at all. Yet I had come up with absolutely nothing, and I felt drained of any more ideas. Feeling too stubborn to totally give up, I had to believe that Ryan's birthmother was somewhere just waiting to be found…by me! I did not have a "plan B," so I would have to think hard about what to do next. To my surprise and absolute delight, the very task I decided to do next would indeed prove to be very fruitful.

Thus far, I had been extremely methodical about where I was searching, keeping lists of who and where I had written and listing the responses I received.

Later on one particular day I felt a little whimsical. I decided to just "play" around on the internet, and I typed in Ryan's birthmother's name on every search engine I could find. Suddenly one item appeared which was a genealogical family group sheet listing a husband, wife, and their children. The husband's or children's names did not mean anything to my search. The wife's name was listed as Joyce Amanda Carter and had a birth date in the late forties.

It was the same first and last name as Ryan's birthmother, and her date of birth matched my initial information. I knew from my previous searches there probably were quite a few persons in the United States named Joyce Carter. I had found that out by contacting quite a few of them, although none turned out to be the one I was looking for. This sheet had more information on the husband, his birth place and date, and their marriage date and place, which was in California. In addition their children's names, dates and places of birth were also listed in California. The whole family was listed in California, the exact opposite coast from New York.

Could it be possible this was the Joyce Carter I was looking for? Could she have moved from New York to California and now had this family? This would mean that years ago both Ryan and his mother had moved from New York City, and now both may be living in California. What a coincidence! I had to talk myself into not becoming too excited about this and being patient, which was not one of my best traits. A lot more investigating would be necessary before I could or should reach any conclusions. It just seemed to me that it was too far-fetched, although I also knew when a person searches for family information surprises seem to turn up. I had learned this when I did my own family genealogy. I kept on searching intensively, still having no luck finding any further information using her maiden name and birthday. I spent the next several months contemplating whether I should heed the words of the person at the National Archives when I visited there, or still plod along trying to figure out what my next strategy was going to be. My decision was to keep plodding along in the search.

Chapter Four

For the next year, I spent more time thinking about my search than actually doing something, since I was rather at a loss of what to do next. Then one day an email surprised me. It was a response to a message I had placed on a genealogical bulletin board some time ago from a person who I did not even know (and still don't)! This person told me to go to a particular website. That was it. No explanation of why or what I would find. I did this and saw it was a company which developed websites for other companies.

At first I thought it was just an effort to advertise their own website business and an attempt at a sales pitch. I stared at this and could not figure out what it all meant.

Then I noticed way down in the lower left corner a small box with a name matching the last name of the husband who had appeared on the sheet I found months before. He was listed as the husband of Joyce Carter. A link appeared in the box. I clicked on it. What appeared was a total surprise! There was the exact same genealogical sheet I had found months ago; however, this time connected to it was a photo of three persons. This time I decided there was no way I could ignore the information. Maybe I could work at researching the other names on this sheet in order to find out more about the spouse named Joyce Carter. I wanted to at the very least verify some kind of connection.

Maybe even embrace the slight possibility that this could be the person I was looking for, who was born on the east coast, lived in New York City, and moved to the west coast…just like Ryan. I never told Ryan about this possible discovery, reminding myself that it probably was too far-fetched to think his birthmother was now living in the same state as he was, on the opposite coast on which they both were born. What were the chances of that?

For a couple of months I constantly searched over any California information I could find, trying to locate any of the person's names listed on that family sheet. I tried California telephone and address listings on the internet. I even called information in some cities, asking for phone numbers for anyone by any of those names; however, I had no luck at all. There just had to be something or someone somewhere who could provide me with information. Deciding to get more aggressive, I went back to that company's website page I had found and nervously emailed one of the company's executive persons listed on the page. I really was not too anxious yet to let anybody know who I was looking for or why; nonetheless, I decided it was worth taking a chance. I emailed a question as to how I could locate the woman listed as the wife on the genealogical sheet connected to that website, stating I wanted to contact the person named Joyce Carter. To my great surprise, I received an email back giving me her personal email address and verifying her name was now Joyce Carter Harwin. Now I was really getting nervous! I would be able to actually correspond with this person, who could possibly prove to be Ryan's birthmother. I asked myself if I was I getting too hopeful. It took me a week to get up the courage and figure out exactly what I was going to say. I still did not want to state what my specific purpose was, in case this might not happen to be the right person. Yet, I did not want to scare her off if indeed it was the right person. I was involved in truly very private information which I felt I could not give out just to anyone. I would have to choose my words carefully.

A long week later, after mulling over what I would do or say, I was at my computer, emailing her. I asked that she pardon the intrusion and told her I was sorry to bother her and I was working on some genealogy for a friend who had lost track of his relatives. I went on to say in his family tree information, there was the name

Joyce Carter, who was born in the forties. All I knew was this Joyce may have lived in New York City at least in the sixties and she was Caucasian, Protestant, and of Danish descent, and may have been a hotel receptionist at one time in New York City. Her mother had died in the sixties. Her father was a retired fireman around that time. I added if she was not this person or did not know of this person I was very sorry to bother her and would not ever bother her again. Now I sat and waited nervously, thinking here was my chance to really find out if this person was indeed Ryan's birthmother. I anxiously waited for any response, not expecting one very soon or maybe not at all.

Chapter Five

Within twenty-four hours I received a response stating I had a good part of the information right. Along with what seemed to be angry-toned comments saying she could not imagine where I would have obtained such personal information and she wanted to know where and how I obtained it! Her first concern was that this information was going over the internet and maybe could be used by an unknown third party in some illegal or harmful way. Her second concern was how I or anyone came by the information I possessed about her, since she was not aware those records would be public. She also admitted she was somewhat frightened I may wish to harm her or wanted to sell this information to someone else. Questioning the honesty of what I was searching for, she wanted me to tell her now what my purpose was.

Waiting until the next day, I was even more nervous. I bravely emailed her back, asking her to tell me which details I had correct. I added that my friend had some additional very detailed information which was found in some papers regarding medical information which could possibly be helpful as well as serve as a definite deciding factor as to whether she was actually the Joyce Carter I was really looking for. That further medical information was the Joyce I was looking for was prone to sinus infections and had a chronic condition of asthma. She also had her tonsils out at age seven and had knee surgery on her right knee at age seventeen years old. Her blood type was B positive.

The quick response I received was not at all a kind one. However, I could hardly blame her. I knew medical information, which should always be held in high confidence, was very personal and there are protective laws against leaking it. Of course, she had no idea where I obtained this information. She stated, again in an angry tone, that she felt very uncomfortable giving out her personal information over the web, especially to strangers.

Furthermore, she went on to tell me that at this time she would refuse to verify any of my information or answer any of my questions. She also wanted to know what relationship the person I was doing this for was claiming to be to her and also where I would have obtained any personal medical records. She insisted I identify myself and the person I was "helping."

I, too, was upset, since if she was annoyed and irritated, I didn't know how she would take the truth as to what all I did know. Yet I could not take the chance of giving out any more information or the real reason for my search. I nervously waited three days trying to figure out what I should do and how I should handle it. I could possibly lose my chance altogether to find out if she was any kind of connection to Ryan.

In the end, I decided not to take any chances in revealing the truth just yet. I emailed her back asking her to accept my humblest apologies for contacting her without much explanation. I told her I, too, was somewhat fearful of having too much information at the mercy of others, especially on the internet.

That was the reason I wanted to confirm who she was before I explained fully. I went on to explain the reason I wanted to be extremely careful was because I needed to make sure she was the right person. The several last details regarding specific health facts could be the assurance I needed. I added that I wanted to also make sure whenever and whatever information I emailed to her, she would be able to view privately and would be read only by her. I told her if she said it was okay to send the last further details, I would do so.

She surprised me with a quick response. She did not think any concerns and information received by her would be a problem, adding there was no doubt she was the person I was looking for! I was joyous beyond words!

I had actually found Ryan's birthmother. Reminding myself not to get too happy, I thought ahead as to how she might react to the fact I was about to tell her that I was working with the son she had given birth to and had given up for adoption.

Would she really want to know about him?

Chapter Six

The ultimate moment had come, and I felt there was no other choice except to let Joyce know what my true purpose was. My next email to her began with the fact that I honestly did not mean any harm to her and totally understood her concern, apologizing again for being evasive. I began first by giving her some of my own personal information, thinking perhaps it would help if she knew exactly who I was. I told her my name, age, where I lived, where I worked, and my address and phone number in case she would like to call me. I said "I have three sons, and as a wife and a mother myself, I would not think of being careless with any information I have about you."

Stating that her information was obtained legitimately, I said, "Indeed I had no malicious intentions, nor was I charging anyone for my search," adding, "I need to make sure that you will be the only person who will see this information because of its private nature. However, if you choose not to respond to my email I promise I will not ever bother you again."(This was difficult since I really did not want to let go and give up. Still, I felt I had to promise this.) I meant what I said. Now I was really glad I hadn't told Ryan anything yet. I would have hated to be this close to finding her and then have her not respond. Surely then I would have to disappoint Ryan.

I began to tell her the real story of how I was looking for the birthmother of my son's friend. I explained how my son and Ryan had become friends in Long Beach and my son asked me to help Ryan in trying to search for his birthmother. I had met Ryan and felt he was pretty special and well worth helping. I described him as good natured, intelligent, multi-talented, creative, having a way with words, and had traveled to other countries, climbed mountains, and was trying to find his niche in the world. He said he had been "grappling" with the issue of his adoption since he was eight years old, and he was really anxious to know if he had any family somewhere. I went on to tell her that Ryan at one time had even tried to search for her himself and had made trips to the public library several years ago to see if he could find any other information about his birth; however, it was without any success. He did search the Manhattan phone books around the year of his birth and found a "J. Carter" who was listed only in one phone book as living on the west side. He could not find any more information. Since then he had fervently hoped he could eventually find her. This was on his mind constantly. He learned from the adoption agency that his real name was Daniel Carter. The agency had also told him his birthmother's name, but only his birthfather's first name. Ryan had sent me copies of the adoption agency information he had acquired. I wanted her to know how my search had started and that I had not acquired any illegal records or private information and did not ever intend to. I had only used genealogical research methods, letter writing or use of the internet to guide me in my search. Most importantly, I felt I should not divulge Ryan's birth issue to her before this point, treating it as a genealogical issue, to protect any individuals involved.

I went on to say that on Mother's Day, I had gone to church to light a candle for her, wherever she was. I had told Ryan I would do this each Mother's Day to give him some hope. I had faith that God works in mysterious ways and things happen in God's time, not necessarily in ours. Also just in case I happened to find his birthmother, I asked Ryan beforehand if I could give her his name, address, and telephone number. I wanted to make sure I also asked his permission first. He said that was fine and also the situation was completely up to his birthmother (if I happened to find her); if she did not want any involvement or wanted to wait a while or connect by phone or letters first, or not at all, that would be okay too. However she might feel, he would respect her feelings. I went on to tell her actually the way I received information was through a genealogical website. I did not even know the person who had directed me to the page with her husband's family tree and genealogical information. I had posted search questions about names and dates, yet never anything specific about Ryan's birth. The reason I did not want to reveal all the information I had was for the exact reasons she had stated. I did not want the information to get into the wrong hands or be used by anyone in a bad way, so I had to first make sure I was connecting to the right individual.

That was it. I had told her all I knew and all I had been searching for. Again I asked her to please accept my apology for any concern on her part that I caused by not explaining all this at the beginning. My last comment was that I had not yet told Ryan anything. If she did not want me to tell him, I would comply with her wishes. This was Ryan's and my agreement, and I gave her Ryan's address and phone number. Now all I could do was wait anxiously for what I hoped would be her reply.

Chapter Seven

I suspected Ryan's birthmother may not respond to me. To my surprise and joy she did. She not only verified the information I had given to her, but added further details which matched ones I had not even mentioned to her, such as her blood type, that she had her tonsils out when she was seven years old, and her adopted mother was deceased. She said she had forgotten what may have been on the adoption form she had to fill out, although she figured some of these details may further prove she really was who I had thought she was. Seemingly genuinely excited because I knew Ryan, she told me her husband and her sister had known about the birth; but her two children did not know at this point. She was planning on telling them that day. She gave me her email address, home address, and phone number, all in a small town in northern California. Needless to say, I was ecstatic. Here she was, not in New York or even on the East Coast, but instead in a small town in northern California, still quite a ways from where Ryan lived now.

She told me she would be quite interested in corresponding with Ryan, but she was a notoriously bad letter writer and not often near a phone. Due to her job, she worked late; therefore, Ryan should probably count on using email rather than the phone. I assured her I would relay all of this information to Ryan.

Anxious to contact Ryan, I immediately phoned him. There was no answer.

I called my son to see if he knew where Ryan was. He then gave me Ryan's cell phone number which I immediately dialed.

When Ryan answered, I asked him where he was at the moment. He told me he was touring some people at his place of work. I figured it was not a good time to talk to him. I asked him if he could call me as soon as he was done with the tour. I couldn't help myself and added since he was closer to my son's apartment than his own, he could go there and I would have some great news for him. When he got there I told him to go on my son's computer, and he would be able to go online to see a picture of his birthmother. He was awkwardly silent for a long time and added, "You're kidding, aren't you?" to which I replied, "Ryan, I would not kid about this. I really did find your birthmother. Believe it or not she lives in California now too, way up north." Ryan was stunned. I told him which website to go to. He could not believe his eyes. His birthmother was on the screen in the photo. Tears began to run down my face because he sounded so happy. I proceeded to tell him some of the details of my search and gave him his birthmother's name, address, phone number, and her email address. For me it was almost as exciting as actually giving birth myself!

Two days later Ryan emailed me and sent me a copy of the email he sent to his birthmother. He told me, in his unusual way with words, "the die is cast" and he would keep me informed as to what might transpire between the two of them. He was eternally grateful to me and considered this a "miraculous" discovery. Ryan had told his birthmother this was a tremendous moment in both their lives. He was virtually speechless, which was "rare" for him, he added. He also had told his birthmother he would like her to know he was happy and healthy, and he was sure her decision to give him up for adoption thirty-four years ago was not an easy one, adding that she should know the folks who raised him were wonderful, giving, and loving people who provided a wonderful home for him. Ryan went on to say he was comfortable with whatever method and pace of communication she chose. He would respect her boundaries and the fact that she had a complete and separate life and family now, who may or may not be aware of his existence. He ended with the fact that he was really looking forward to hearing from her and gave her his personal email address.

After a little over a year and a half, my search had ended. Both Ryan and I had gained a great gift from our journey. His was an end to a long search, and mine was the ability to give that to him. I was extremely glad it ended happily. I said a special prayer and lit a candle for this.

In the days to come, Ryan and his birthmother continued to correspond, mainly through email, which was convenient for both of them. He was kind enough to actually copy some of those emails to me so I could read them.

She told him he was a "beautiful baby" and explained to him her circumstances at the time of his birth. Giving him up for adoption was a very difficult decision, she said, but it was only made easier because she knew of no way that a child could successfully grow up in the sort of poverty she was in at the time. She also expressed sadness that both his adoptive parents had passed away and wanted to know as much as she could about them.

Ryan also learned he had many aunts and cousins, in addition to the half-brother and half-sister who were very soon going to know of his existence.

His birthmother, after seeing an emailed photo of Ryan, concluded that he had a great resemblance to her father, Ryan's maternal grandfather. She also said this was the biggest news to hit the family in years. Everyone was excited to hear about him and see the photo. His mother filled him with a myriad of information about what she had done with her life after Ryan's birth, what her husband and children were like, and what all their interests were. She even told him about the Danish heritage of her family, in which Ryan was very much interested.

I had noticed his birthmother had the same trait of using a lot of different words in unusual and interesting ways, just as Ryan did. Another surprise was in the email Ryan received from his birthmother, she frequently mentioned some of her ventures into nature, the trees, archeology, and Indian basketry she liked. It suddenly struck me when hearing this, it was the connection to the basket laying on Ryan's desk that he and I had talked about, which was filled with furnishings from nature such as feathers, natural pieces of wood, and some Indian artifacts. We had somehow known there was a connection, and there it was!

She always signed her email with "love to you," which made me feel glad for Ryan. They seemed to correspond frequently with ease. Both had a lot of questions for the other.

Ryan was very grateful he was what he called "openly received," since he had in the past heard a few nightmare stories of found families. I had heard some of these too; therefore I will be eternally grateful that the search for Ryan's birthmother turned out the way it did.

In the months that followed, Ryan corresponded with his birthmother quite frequently through email as well as talked to her on the phone once in a while. Eventually he and his mother met for the first time in San Diego where Ryan was running in a marathon. His mother agreed to wait at the finish line, which is where they both laid eyes on each other for the very first time.

During one conversation, Ryan cautiously asked about his birthfather. She gave him some sketchy information; however, it was never enough to really let him know very much, and she told him his father "was unaware of her pregnancy," the same words we both had seen on the papers from the adoption agency. Later, Ryan and I were to find out quite differently.

Chapter Eight

"I'll bet it is strange, not searching for Carters anymore." This was the first sentence in an email I received from Ryan the next fall. He also mentioned the possibility of a new search we could do for his biological father.

I could tell that Ryan was getting more and more curious about who his birthfather was. To tell the truth, I felt the same way, although didn't want to say too much to him about this. My instinct kept telling me it may be even easier to find his birthfather. All Ryan knew other than what he had read on his birth record, was from the information his birthmother had given him. It seemed evident she didn't necessarily want to give him very much information, only that his birthfather's first name was Joel and he had been a student at New York University. She had added he "did not want to be involved" with Ryan's birth. She went on to tell Ryan that, although they did part friends, she had never seen him since Ryan's birth. And if he had chosen to become involved, she probably would not have placed Ryan up for adoption. His birthfather had come to the hospital and "grinned all over" when he saw Ryan. She described him as tall, with wavy hair and a mustache, brown eyes, and of English descent. She said that he was from Tappan, New York, was soft spoken, a lot of fun, read a lot and wrote poetry, and could not cook. He worked and went to school. None of these items could serve very well as clues to finding him, except probably the Tappan, New York, location, which I for one had never heard of.

Ryan reassured me he was not trying to push me into searching again, except he was just curious as to whether it might be possible to find him. Little did Ryan know it would only take one slight gentle nudge for me to get all excited about beginning the search for his birthfather. When he emailed me about it, I immediately said "I thought you would never ask; absolutely, the search is on!" Ryan emailed me he too was truly excited about the search for his birthfather, saying it was time for me to light some candles again. I certainly did. Could I possibly dare to hope I could be successful in finding his birthfather? Well, here I was, again looking over all the information on Ryan's thirty-four-year-old papers he had obtained from the adoption agency.

What I already knew about his birthfather was he had at that time been in his early twenties and single; he was Protestant, Caucasian, of English heritage, born and raised in the United States; he was of average weight; he had auburn hair, blue eyes, and a fair complexion; he was employed with IBM and was a college student majoring in literature; he was one of three children in his family; he came from a wealthy family background; and of course, as we were told, he "was unaware of the pregnancy." (At least that's what the papers had stated.)

With these facts, the only detail I could figure out was that Ryan's birthfather, first name Joel, was born in the forties. I already knew from the papers that his birthfather's parents (who would be Ryan's grandparents) had been a postmaster and a psychologist. This again brought up the usual question of where to start searching. I had no last name. Most likely there were quite a few IBM workers or literature majors at Columbia University with the common name Joel. I really did not even know if he actually ever graduated from the university.

I needed a last name for Joel. The only way I thought I might find it (since Ryan's birthmother did not volunteer this information and seemed hesitant to do so) was to work from the fact that his father had been a postmaster in the sixties in Tappan, New York.

The postal service must keep a record of all the past postmasters, I thought, and I knew the year. I began once again looking on the internet for persons on genealogical websites who may have some connection to that mysterious town of Tappan, New York, and perhaps could try to find out for me who the postmaster was during the sixties.

In the meantime I had posted the following inquiry on some of the genealogy sites which I found on the internet.

"Looking for information on a postmaster in Tappan, New York (Rockland County) in the sixties. Want to know who he was and if he had a son named Joel who attended Columbia University in sixties, majoring in literature (he also worked at IBM while in college). His mother may have been a psychologist in the sixties."

I also sent Ryan a copy of this in case he would run across any further information.

And then the wait began!

Chapter Nine

While I waited for any information to come my way by any means, I continued to explore on the internet and go to genealogy websites.

I did find a person on one genealogy website who actually lived in the town of Tappan, living there for the last sixteen years. He didn't know any of the previous postmasters at the local post office. However, he was kind enough to give me the current postmaster's name and a phone number so I could call him. He also gave me the name and address of a current college professor who was a lifelong resident of Tappan and was "a great student of local history" in case I might want to contact him to see if he had any information.

To my surprise, I received an email from another genealogy group person online stating that he himself was from Tappan. He could not remember who the postmaster was in the sixties. He had called the Tappan Post Office and was told no one could remember who the postmaster was then. The post office suggested to him that he call someone named Vern, the postmaster of another post office in one of the adjacent communities. He made the call and emailed me back, saying they thought it may have been a person named Frank Maseck, although this was not for sure. He gave me the phone number and said I could call Vern in a couple of days to give him time to check further. I did just that. When I called him back, he said he thought the postmaster had been instead a person named Wes Porter. It was a long shot; still, I had a name I could maybe work on.

I thought maybe if I could find the female psychologist's name it would lead me to match that last name with the last name of the postmaster. Maybe this would confirm what the last name really was.

On one of the genealogy websites, I had placed an inquiry asking if there was anyone who had access to a sixties Tappan, New York phone directory and could look up in the yellow pages to see if there were any female psychologists listed and their names. In response, a person contacted me and suggested I write to the Chamber of Commerce and ask them, or maybe contact the American Medical Association in case there would have been a list of doctors and psychologists practicing at that time. I pondered on those suggestions, thinking they might be worth a try.

In mid-fall, another person who saw my inquiry on the internet emailed me and told me about the Tappan Historical Society, giving me a lady's name and address who was involved with the society as well as with the local Tappan Library and the phone numbers. He also gave me the phone number of the clerk's office in a nearby town, telling me perhaps someone in that town might remember. He thought the name I may be looking for was Blauevelt, who had strong roots in that adjacent town. He also told me there was a man named Pete Malter in Tappan who owned an antique shop next to the public library who was very active in Tappan history and a member of the historical society.

I had certainly obtained quite a few names and connections in Tappan, but still nothing seemed to fit with what I was looking for. I marveled at how I could be fortunate in finding such people willing to help and really appreciated them, yet I didn't even know them.

I spent the entire winter searching for any clue or connection I could find. In the meantime I had sent Ryan a copy of the information I had posted on one of the genealogy sites:

"Looking for information on a Weston Porter family; I think he was a postmaster in Tappan, New York (Rockland County) in the sixties. Want to know if he had three children, especially a son named Joel who attended Columbia University in the sixties, majoring in literature (he also worked at IBM while in college). His mother may have been a psychologist in 1960s."

My hope was one of us, Ryan or me, would run across any other information which may give us some more direction in our search. Spring was coming soon. Maybe with spring would come something new and exciting for my search. I could only hope.

Chapter Ten

Spring came around the next year when Ryan and I got somewhat of an unexpected jolt! His birthmother had sent him an email saying she was quite upset. Someone she knew had seen a posting on a genealogical website saying that I was searching for a Weston Porter. Lucky for us it was the first time she did confirm for Ryan and me the person was indeed his grandfather, and the son Joel was his birthfather. We had a name! I could hardly contain myself, even though his birthmother was concerned about any search for him, stating only because she gave him her word to protect his privacy.

She did tell Ryan it was okay with her if we continued to search for him, even telling Ryan to say hello to him if we found him, making sure he knew she did not "violate her word." Ryan told me that we were now "in the clear" and could continue with our search for his birthfather.

Now I could go back to that same Wes Porter name I was not sure had any meaning at the time and follow the lead to find his son Joel, Ryan's birthfather.

The helpful person in Tappan had mentioned a Wes Porter, and here we were on the right trail!

A few weeks later the "icing was on the cake." I received a nice email note from Pete Malter, stating:

"Sorry to have been tardy in replying to your requests re: Joel. I'll show your letter to the Tappantown Historical Society and possibly a clue may surface.

This is the current address of Weston Porter: postmaster in 1960s, 503 Baywood Drive South, Dunedine, Florida, 33128 or 33528.

Respectfully, Pete."

It was Porter. "Eureka," I squealed to myself. I had found Ryan's paternal grandfather and even had a current address. I immediately emailed Ryan with the news. He emailed back saying his birthmother had confirmed his birthfather was indeed Joel Porter. She met him in Pearl River, New York (Rockland County) where she was working as a clerk around the time she met Joel. Ryan stated this was "amazing and exciting to say the least."

My next move was to decide how to approach telling the Mr. Weston Porter, the grandfather, that I was looking for his son. Next, something happened to really catch me off guard. I had just come home from shopping when my husband met me at the door with a big grin on his face. I asked what the matter was. He told me I had better listen to the answering machine.

The phone had rung, and he did not get to it on time. There was a message left for me. I asked who it was. He said, "I think it is Ryan's father!"

Shocked, I said "This cannot be." I had not even found him yet and just recently found Ryan's grandfather, who did not even know who I was. My husband smiled and said, "Just go listen."

As I listened I was astounded at what I heard. A male voice said his name was Joel Porter and his father, who lived in Florida, had told him I was looking for him. He left his phone number, asking me to call him. I was stunned and shaken to say the least. I wanted to call him back right away; however, I needed to quickly figure out how I could gently explain why I was looking for him. I nervously decided to make the call right away. He answered, telling me he understood I was looking for him, and I could only nervously blurt out one sentence. "Do you know you have a son?" I said. Ryan's father, in a very calm voice, answered "Yes, I thought this might be about him." Somehow the word had reached Mr. Weston Porter, retired postmaster in Florida, that some strange lady in the Midwest was looking for his son. He went on to tell me he had been there at Ryan's birth, holding him moments afterward. The only reason he left was because Ryan's mother did not want to get married or keep the baby, and the adoption agency would not let him keep the baby even though he wanted to. That was the last time he had seen Ryan. In the last few years he had experienced a longing to try to find him.

He was absolutely ecstatic Ryan was found! He said Ryan's grandfather in Florida had also been extremely anxious to find Ryan.

Ryan's birthfather had never married and now lived in a small town in Washington State, which was another surprise. He had left the east coast and moved to the west coast just as Ryan and his birthmother had, none of them knowing about each other. Giving me his address and phone number, he told me he was thankful I found him, and I could have Ryan call him. He added that he had diabetes, had a leg amputation, and lived by himself in a trailer but he had traveled extensively. I could not wait to contact Ryan. I must admit after the phone call from Ryan's birthfather, tears came streaming down my face once again. I immediately called Ryan and told him the second good news. Both of us were ecstatic, to say the least!

Chapter Eleven

My journey was over. What a journey it had been! That summer, I received a very nice thank you card written together by Ryan and his father:

Dear Lynn,

I have spent many wonderful hours…wonderful, wonderful hours, traveling, talking, sharing, getting to know my father, and it has been a gift on so many levels. I have the deepest gratitude for your persistence in bringing us together. The journey continues, and you are in our hearts. Lots of love, Ryan.

Thank you and know that you are in my prayers now, too, for this most precious gift you've given me and Ryan. We've just spent an especially close and rewarding afternoon together sharing our separated lives with one another. We met in the Redwood Forest on Friday and have been traveling together for a couple of days now, each better than the last, and still a couple more to go (for this first reunion, the first of many I believe). Thank you with all my heart. We send our love and gratitude.

Love, Ryan's father.

Tears filled my eyes once again, and I felt as if I also had received a gift of enormous proportion which could never be measured. The search for his birthparents had ended, and now Ryan could start a new beginning learning to know both of them. It would be another adventure for him and without separated lives!

Epilogue

During the writing of this book, Ryan was able to spend time with both his birthparents. He grew to know their present-day families and found out he also had other relatives whom he never knew about before. A wonderful connection was also made with his paternal grandfather in Florida, and in fact, Ryan and his wife and first child moved to the same town in Florida to be closer to his paternal grandfather. However, it was unfortunate that Ryan's father passed away shortly after they met several times, and Ryan had to be the one to take care of his father's belongings, which included some writings his father left behind. I am certain he will cherish these, and they will live on in a special way in Ryan's heart.

Ryan now has a wife and two children and lives in Los Angeles, California.

9 781639 455485